Rage!

A Play by Anthony Masters

Illustrated by Paul Nicholls

Series Editors: Steve Barlow and Steve Skidmore

Heinemann

Published by Heinemann Educational Publishers
Halley Court, Jordan Hill, Oxford OX2 8EJ
A division of Reed Educational and Professional Publishing Ltd

OXFORD MELBOURNE AUCKLAND
JOHANNESBURG BLANTYRE GABORONE
IBADAN PORTSMOUTH NH (USA) CHICAGO

First published 2000
2004 2003 2002 2001
10 9 8 7 6 5 4 3 2
ISBN 0 435 21405 5

Illustrations by Paul Nicholls
Cover design by Shireen Nathoo Design
Cover artwork by Mark Edwards
Designed by Artistix, Thame, Oxon
Printed and bound in Great Britain by Biddles Ltd

Tel: 01865 888058 www.heinemann.co.uk

Contents

Characters

Charlie is tall, well-built and good at football.

Dawn is Charlie's girlfriend.

Darren is one of Charlie's football team mates.

Wayne Williams is a player on another team.

Coach is the coach of the football team. He is also leader of the youth club.

Tracy is Dawn's friend.

The **Mugger** is a young teenager.

Scene One

The sports club

In the snack bar of the sports club. Charlie Brent is waiting near the door to the sports hall. He is wearing jeans, trainers and a shirt. Dawn, Tracy and Darren are playing pool. Wayne Williams comes through the door carrying his football kit. Charlie moves to block his way.

CHARLIE: I want a word with you, Williams.

WILLIAMS: Oh yeah?

CHARLIE: You nearly took my legs off in that match just now.

WILLIAMS: That's not how the ref saw it.

CHARLIE: Then you got *me* sent off.

(Charlie's team coach comes in. Charlie and Wayne don't see him. He stands watching them.)

WILLIAMS: You got yourself sent off, pal. Taking a swing like that. Naughty, naughty boy.

CHARLIE: You think you've got away with it. Don't worry. I'll have you.

WILLIAMS: You know your trouble, mate? You haven't got enough sense to mug blokes when the ref isn't looking. You're a nutter.

(Charlie roars in rage and goes to grab Wayne. He is held back by the coach.)

COACH: You're out, Charlie.

WILLIAMS: Charlie's having another go at me.

CHARLIE: Williams was bugging me.

COACH: I've told you before. Leave it to the ref. And as for you, Williams – leg it, like now.

(Williams goes away.)

COACH: How many more matches is your temper going to lose for us?

CHARLIE: The ref was out of order.

COACH: That's what they all say. That's what you always say. As soon as I find a replacement, you're history.

CHARLIE: You're going to drop me? Oh, come on! Be fair.

COACH: *(Walking back into the club)* I'm being fair, Charlie. Think about it. Sort yourself out. Or take up another sport. Why don't you try tiddlywinks?

CHARLIE: Fair? You don't know what fair means.

(As Coach leaves, Dawn comes over. She is worried.)

DAWN: So you lost your cool. Again. When are you going to learn, Charlie?

CHARLIE: That guy Williams got to me. He kept winding me up. All the way through the game.

DAWN: And you smacked him one – right in the middle of the pitch. Dead clever!

CHARLIE: He was well out of order.

DAWN: Everyone's out of order to you. Everybody who doesn't agree with Charlie Brent. You laid one on a player in the other team. You got sent off. End of story.

CHARLIE: I lost my temper. That's all. Everyone loses their cool once in a while.

DAWN: You can do it once too often. Now you've been dumped. Right?

CHARLIE: They can't do that. I'm the best man on the field.

DAWN: They've had enough of you. Like I have. In fact I'm up to here with it all. You really fancy yourself, don't you? And you don't learn.

CHARLIE: What do you mean by that?

DAWN: I mean I've had enough, Charlie.

CHARLIE: You're saying we're finished ...

DAWN: How many more times do I have to tell you?

CHARLIE: You've dumped me for someone else, haven't you? Who's the lucky boy then?

DAWN: Darren asked me to go clubbing on Saturday.

CHARLIE: That idiot? Good luck. He dances like his pants are on fire.

DAWN: At least he shows me a bit of respect.

CHARLIE: I'll give him a bit of respect. You see if I don't.

DAWN: See? That's what I mean! You think you can sort out everything with your fists, don't you?

CHARLIE: Darren! He can't dance, can't play footy...

DAWN: I don't go out with boys just because they're good at football and dancing. I go out with someone I can respect.

CHARLIE: We'll see about that.

DAWN: I'm going to talk to Tracy. She's more fun than you. In fact you're no fun at all. Talking to you is like talking to a brick wall.

CHARLIE: Why don't you go and talk to Tracy then? Just push off!

(Charlie walks across the floor to where Darren is playing pool.)

CHARLIE: I want you – outside.

DARREN: *(Lining up a shot)* What for?

CHARLIE: We need to talk about Dawn.

DARREN: You're putting me off my game.

CHARLIE: I'll put you off more than that.

DARREN: I don't get you. What are you so worked up about?

CHARLIE: I don't want you seeing Dawn. So lay off her, or I'll break your legs.

DARREN: *(Still lining up his shot)* Why don't you just get lost. Go somewhere else. Take a trip to Planet Zeron.

CHARLIE: Make me.

DARREN: I don't sort things out like that.

CHARLIE: How do you sort things out then?

DARREN: It's a free world. Dawn can go out with who she likes.

CHARLIE: But not with a wimp like you.

DARREN: *(Slowly putting down his cue)* Who says I'm a wimp? Maybe I should come outside and smack you one.

CHARLIE: Who's the hard man now then?

DARREN: We can soon find out.

(Seeing trouble, Dawn and Tracy come across.)

DAWN: What's going on?

CHARLIE: Not a lot. Yet.

DARREN: There's nothing I can't handle.

CHARLIE: You sure about that?

DAWN: You're sick, Charlie. You just can't stand losing face, can you?

CHARLIE: Losing you isn't losing face.

DARREN: Watch your mouth, Charlie. Dawn's worth two of you.

DAWN: Leave it out, Darren.

DARREN: I'm not leaving out anything.

TRACY: Look, why don't we all back off? Charlie, come and have a drink. Darren – finish your game.

CHARLIE: If I was going to have a drink I'd have a real drink. *(He grabs the cue and crashes it down on the snooker table.)* I don't want any kids' drinks.

DAWN: Go and drink what you like. Just get out of my face.

CHARLIE: OK, Darren, why don't we settle this outside? Just the two of us.

DARREN: Why not then?

DAWN: No way.

TRACY: Leave it out, both of you. There's no point in ...

CHARLIE: You keep out of it. Now are you coming outside, Darren?

DARREN: Too right I am.

DAWN: Come on, Tracy, let's leave them to it.

(Dawn moves away towards the soft drinks bar while the boys walk to the door. From the bar, Dawn has a view of the street.)

DAWN: Charlie!

CHARLIE: What is it? Changed your mind, have you?

DAWN: That old woman. Some kid's grabbed her handbag. She's just been mugged.

CHARLIE: *(Running to the door)* I'll sort it.

DAWN: That could be difficult.

CHARLIE: Why?

DAWN: That mugger's gone off on your new mountain bike.

CHARLIE: He won't get away with that. I'll take him apart.

(He dashes outside.)

DARREN: Say what you like, Charlie isn't fussy. He'll hit anybody.

TRACY: Charlie always means business. He'll sort it.

DAWN: At least the woman's OK. There's a crowd round her now.

DARREN: I'm going after Charlie. He might need some help.

DAWN: You'll have a job doing that.

DARREN: Why?

DAWN: Charlie's just ridden off on *your* bike.

DARREN: He can't do that.

DAWN: He's done it.

DARREN: We'd better go after him.

TRACY: He'll be all right.

DARREN: It's not him I'm worried about. What happens if he catches that mugger? He's going to kill somebody one of these days.

DAWN: Come on. I'll give you a lift on my crossbar.

(Dawn drags Darren through the door. Tracy follows them calling:)

TRACY: Hey! Wait for me!

SCENE TWO

At the river

An old bridge over the river. Charlie and the mugger's voices come from off stage, where Charlie is slowly catching up with the young mugger.

CHARLIE: *(Voice off)* I'm going to kill you!

MUGGER: *(Voice off)* No way!

(The mugger rides on and skids to a stop by the bridge. Charlie follows. He gets off his bike and walks slowly towards the mugger.)

CHARLIE: I'm going to break your arms and legs. I'm going to take you apart. I'm going to turn your head the wrong way round. I'm going to change the shape of your face. Your own mother won't know you!

MUGGER: You'll have to catch me first.

(The mugger ducks under a rope and on to the bridge, dragging Charlie's bike with him.)

CHARLIE: Wait up! Can't you read the notice?

MUGGER: What notice?

CHARLIE: It says the bridge isn't safe. It's closed. The river is high. The bridge could fall down at any moment.

MUGGER: That notice has been up there for ever. Bye!

CHARLIE: Give me my bike! If you don't I'll –

MUGGER: Have a nice evening!

(Just then, Dawn and Darren arrive with Tracy close behind. They are on the other side of the bridge.)

CHARLIE: Where have you lot been? Stop for a cup of tea, did you?

DARREN: We lost you. We came by the top road.

CHARLIE: You're just in time to watch this toe-rag being shredded.

DAWN: *(To Tracy)* He's only a young kid!

TRACY: Not too young for Charlie to beat him up!

DAWN: *(Yelling at the mugger)* You've got nowhere to go!

TRACY: We won't hurt you.

CHARLIE: Much!

DARREN: Give up now. It's the only thing you can do.

MUGGER: *(Getting off Charlie's bike)* Is it?

CHARLIE: You're going to get donc so bad …

MUGGER: *(Pushing Charlie's bike towards the side of the bridge)* Just try it! You take another step towards me and I'll throw your bike in the river.

CHARLIE: Then you'll go with it. You don't stand a chance.

DAWN: Stay back, Charlie! He means what he says.

CHARLIE: So do I.

TRACY: Think it out, Charlie. That bike cost you a bomb.

CHARLIE: I've got a right to lose my rag this time.

DARREN: Lose your rag and you'll lose your bike.

MUGGER: Your mates are right. They're talking sense.

CHARLIE: What gives you the right to say that? You granny-bashing little rat bag.

(Slowly, Darren begins to move towards the mugger who turns round just in time.)

MUGGER: And don't you try nothing, either.

CHARLIE: Darren – you keep back.

MUGGER: Now you're talking sense.

CHARLIE: You're scared, aren't you?

MUGGER: Me? No chance.

CHARLIE: You're scared you're going to be nicked.

MUGGER: You're scared your bike is going in the river.

CHARLIE: Your hands are shaking.

MUGGER: So's your bike.

(For a moment Charlie seems about to make a rush at the mugger. Then Charlie relaxes.)

CHARLIE: Okay. It's a stand-off. Let's talk.

MUGGER: What about?

CHARLIE: Let's talk about losing.

MUGGER: Losing what? A bike?

CHARLIE: You can lose all kinds of stuff. I just lost a match.

MUGGER: Weren't there any more in the matchbox?

CHARLIE: A football match, you thick idiot.

MUGGER: Rubbish player, are you?

CHARLIE: I'm good.

MUGGER: So how come you lost the match?

CHARLIE: I broke the rules. Just like you've done.

MUGGER: Don't give me that.

CHARLIE: I just did.

MUGGER: Rules are for prats.

CHARLIE: That's what I thought. So I smacked another player.

MUGGER: That was stupid.

CHARLIE: You're right. I got dumped from the team and I lost my girlfriend. But you broke the rules too. Stealing's against the law. Didn't you know that?

MUGGER: What's your girlfriend like then?

DAWN: She was fantastic. Real looker.

MUGGER: So how come you lost out on her?

CHARLIE: I was stupid.

MUGGER: You look it.

CHARLIE: She walked out on me. *(He glances across the bridge at Dawn)*

MUGGER: Why did she do that?

CHARLIE: Because I kept losing my temper.

TRACY: *(To the mugger)* Give Charlie back his bike.

MUGGER: Let me go and I'll leave it outside the station.

DARREN: Promises, promises.

CHARLIE: You're not going anywhere.

MUGGER: Just tell your mates to back off. If they don't, I'll give you ten seconds.

CHARLIE: And then?

MUGGER: Your bike goes in the river. I'm counting. One. Two –

CHARLIE: You chuck my bike in and –

MUGGER: Tell them to back off.

CHARLIE: No chance.

MUGGER: Three. Four. Five –

DARREN: Don't do it. It'll only go worse for you in court.

MUGGER: What do I care? It's going to go bad for me anyway. I'm still counting. Six. Seven –

(Charlie gets ready to rush at the mugger. But, with great effort, he controls himself.)

CHARLIE: What's your name?

MUGGER: I'm not telling you.

CHARLIE: I've got to call you something.

MUGGER: I don't want you to call me anything. I promise you – this bike's going in whatever you do. So tell your mates to let me go.

CHARLIE: No chance.

MUGGER: Eight. Nine –

(Charlie ducks under the barrier. He begins to walk slowly towards the teenager.)

MUGGER: You stay back.

CHARLIE: Give me my bike.

TRACY: Give it to him. I've told you before – Charlie's got a temper. He'll beat the hell out of you.

MUGGER: You're out of time.

CHARLIE: So are you.

DAWN: Charlie! No!

(Charlie runs towards the mugger. They have a quick tug of war over the bike. The mugger lets go of the bike, and loses his balance. He falls into the river.)

DAWN: Now you've done it, Charlie. He'll drown.

(Charlie throws his bike to safety and gets ready to jump in.)

DAWN: Don't, Charlie. The current's strong down there. You'll both drown.

(Charlie takes off his trainers.)

DARREN: Don't be a fool. He'll have to take his chances.

TRACY: Leave it, Charlie. You'll get dragged down.

CHARLIE: Look, he'll drown. I've got to get him out of there.

(Charlie jumps off the bridge. Dawn, Tracy and Darren look down into the river.)

DAWN: Charlie's crazy. He's going to be a dead hero. *(She is crying)* Where is he? Darren – where is he? Why don't you tell me?

DARREN: I'm trying to spot him.

DAWN: He's dead, isn't he? He's gone under. He's drowned –

TRACY: *(Holding Dawn)* He'll be all right. Charlie's a strong swimmer.

DAWN: He's drowned, hasn't he. Charlie's drowned.

DARREN: Wait a minute! I can see the mugger. His head's bobbing up and down. There's a lot of white water – hang on! There he is! There's Charlie! He's trying to grab the kid.

DAWN: What's that stupid kid doing?

DARREN: He's punching Charlie. He's trying to push him away.

TRACY: He's mad. Doesn't he want to get rescued?

DARREN: Now Charlie's smacked him. He's got him in a life-saving position. He's pulling the kid towards the bank. There's a lot of white water down there. Hang on –

DAWN: Where are they?

DARREN: They've both gone under again. I can't see either of them. There's so much water.

DAWN: *(Yelling)* Charlie! Oh God! Charlie!

DARREN: OK. Panic over. I can see them again. Nearer the bank this time. Much nearer.

DAWN: There's Charlie!

TRACY: He's made it!

DARREN: Charlie's pulling the kid up on to the bank.

(Charlie climbs up the bank. The others help him drag the mugger up the bank.)

DAWN: Charlie, are you OK?

CHARLIE: I'm fine. I really enjoy a freezing cold swim.

TRACY: *(Reaching in her bag for her mobile)* I'm going to call the police.

CHARLIE: *(To Dawn)* There! See? All right? I didn't beat him up.

DAWN: You still lost it!

CHARLIE: Eh?

DAWN: You had to go and rush him, didn't you?

CHARLIE: Give me a break! I nearly talked him off that bridge.

DAWN: Nearly isn't enough! I thought we'd lost you. I don't want to go through that again. Do you hear me? Not ever!

SCENE THREE

The Match

The football field. A friendly game. Dawn and Tracy are on the touch line. They are standing next to Coach.

COACH: I should never have agreed to let Charlie play today. Wayne Williams is giving him bother again.

DAWN: Williams?

COACH: The guy Charlie hit in the indoor match. Remember? Let's hope he can keep control.

DAWN: *(Yelling)* Charlie! Keep your cool. Don't let Williams wind you up.

TRACY: *(Shouting)* Ooh, that was dirty!

(The referee's whistle blows.)

DAWN: What happened?

COACH: Williams tripped Charlie. Now we've got problems.

DAWN: *(Shouting)* Don't blow it now, Charlie. Remember what happened on the bridge.

COACH: What bridge?

TRACY: The ref's sending Williams off. Or trying to.

DAWN: *(Shouting)* Charlie, don't touch Williams!

COACH: *(To Dawn)* He's not going to. I'd better get Charlie off the pitch and check him over.

(Coach signals Charlie to come off the pitch and Charlie limps towards him.)

COACH: You OK, Charlie?

CHARLIE: Just turned my ankle. I'll be OK in a sec.

(Coach gives Charlie the magic sponge treatment.)

DAWN: Well done, Charlie – you were really cool.

CHARLIE: What?

DAWN: You didn't have a go at Williams.

CHARLIE: Yeah – well – I just thought about what happened at the bridge.

COACH: What's all this about a bridge?

DAWN: It's a long story.

COACH: Fill me in after the game. I reckon you'll do, Charlie. Want to go back on?

DAWN: Charlie – what if we – would you like to –

CHARLIE: Are you giving me another chance?

COACH: What is this, a football match or the Jerry Springer show?

(Dawn kisses Charlie. Coach throws his sponge away in despair.)

TRACY: Way to go, Dawn!

(We hear the referee's whistle as the game restarts.)

COACH: What's got into Charlie? He's acting like he's …

DAWN: In control. Yeah.

COACH: I never thought I'd see it.

DAWN: Are you still going to ban him?

COACH: Not if he keeps this up – yes! Great pass! He's on a run. Come on, Charlie … Foul! Penalty!

(Coach races off along the touchline as the referee's whistle blows.)

TRACY: Dawn …

DAWN: Shurrup! Charlie's going to take the penalty.

TRACY: But, Dawn …

DAWN: What?

TRACY: What about you and Darren?

DAWN: Oh, yeah. I feel bad about Darren. He's going to think I used him.

TRACY: Well, I was going to say – I've had my eye on Darren for some time. And if the coast's clear …

DAWN: It is.

TRACY: I'd like to chance my luck.

DAWN: Ssssh! There he goes … Goal! Charlie's scored!

(The referee's whistle blows full time as they celebrate. Charlie jogs over. As he hugs Dawn, Williams comes over.)

WILLIAMS: I'll get you for this, sunshine.

CHARLIE: Tough luck, pal. You shouldn't have tried to mug me while the ref was looking.

WILLIAMS: You want to get funny? Come on then! Let's sort this out. Right here.

CHARLIE: There's only one place I'm sorting you out.

WILLIAMS: Where's that?

CHARLIE: On the field. Playing the game.

WILLIAMS: Have you gone soft? That doesn't sound like Charlie Brent talking.

CHARLIE: It's the way I sound now. It's the way I'm always gonna sound. Get it?